3

LET'S GO
GRAMMAR
and
LISTENING
Activity Book

Susan Rivers

Oxford University Press

Review

 Listen and choose.

_____a_____ 1. **a.** She's Miss Smith. She's a nurse.

b. He's Mr. Jones. He's a farmer.

_____ 2. **a.** Yes, she is.

b. No, he isn't.

_____ 3. **a.** No, she isn't.

b. They're Mr. and Mrs. Long.
They're teachers.

_____ 4. **a.** Yes, they are.

b. They're cooks.

_____ 5. **a.** They're Susan and Ron.
They're students.

b. She's Rita. She's a student.

 Listen and circle.

1. **a.** Where's the bathtub?

b. Where's the refrigerator?

2. **a.** Are there lamps behind the sofa?

b. Are there lamps behind the stove?

3. **a.** Is the bed in the dining room?

b. Is the bed in the bedroom?

4. **a.** Where's the TV?

b. Where's the sink?

Listen and choose. 🎞

1. __e__	2. _____	3. _____	4. _____
5. _____	6. _____	7. _____	8. _____

a. I have a comic book.

b. Yes, I do.

c. Yes, I can.

d. He has a coin.

e. She can speak English.

f. Yes, he does.

g. He wants a cookie.

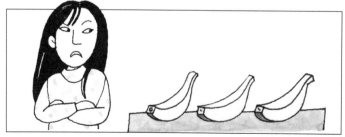

h. No, she doesn't.

Review

Listen and choose. 📼

eats	do	eating	play

does	playing	eat	is	plays

1. She ___eats___ breakfast.

2. He's _____ breakfast.

3. I _____ breakfast.

4. I'm _____ the piano.

5. He _____ the piano.

6. I _____ the piano.

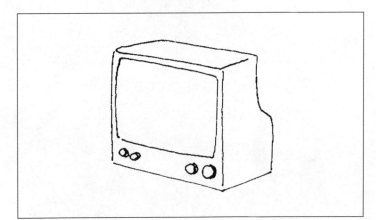

7. Yes, he _____.

8. Yes, she _____.

9. Yes, I _____.

4

Listen and match.

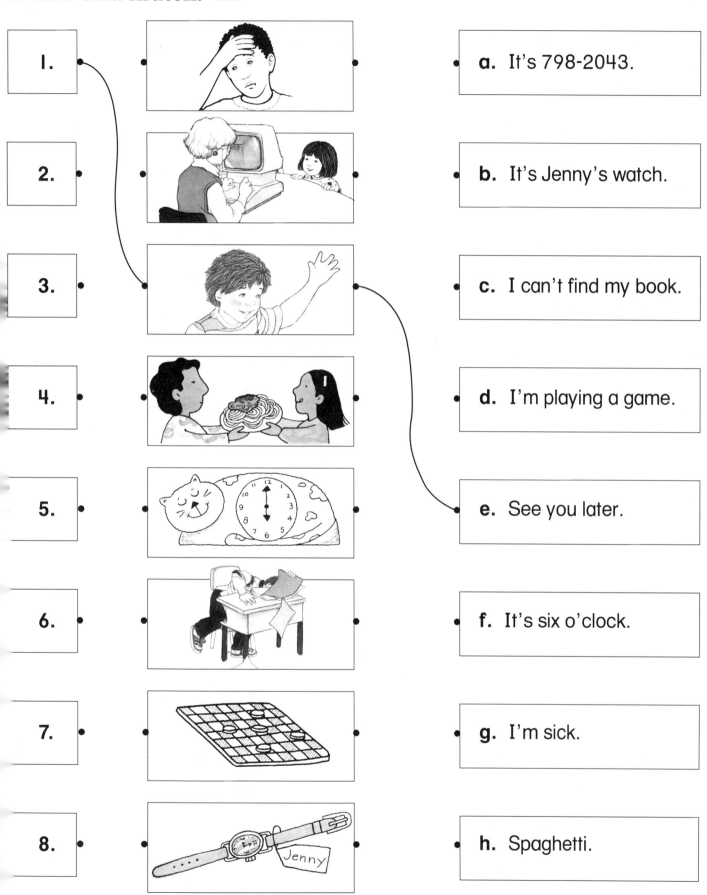

1.

2.

3.

4.

5.

6.

7.

8.

a. It's 798-2043.

b. It's Jenny's watch.

c. I can't find my book.

d. I'm playing a game.

e. See you later.

f. It's six o'clock.

g. I'm sick.

h. Spaghetti.

Review

Listen, fill in the letters, and solve the puzzles.
Then answer the questions. 🔲

1. h   2. ___   3. ___   4. ___   5. ___   6. ___   7. ___

8. ___   9. ___   10. ___   11. ___   12. ___   13. ___   14. ___

15. ___   16. ___   17. ___   18. ___   19. ___   20. ___   21. ___

1. | 1, 7, 6 | | 2, 8, 19 | | 3, 7, 5 |

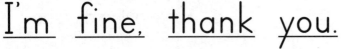

How are you?
I'm fine, thank you.

2. | 6, 1, 19, 8, 19 | | 10, 7 | | 3, 7, 5 | | 11, 20, 18, 19 |

_____ _____ _____ _____?

_____

3. | 6, 1, 2, 13 | | 12, 2, 14 | | 3, 7, 5 | | 10, 7 |

_____ _____ _____ _____?

_____

4. | 10, 7 | | 3, 7, 5 | | 11, 20 ,15, 19 | | 16, 9, 2, 17, 1, 19, 13, 13, 20 |

___ ___ _____ _____?

_____

Listen and choose the word with the different sound.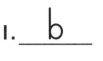

1. __b__   a.    b.    c.

2. _____   a. 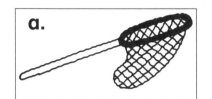   b.    c.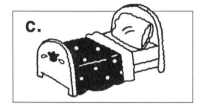

3. _____   a. 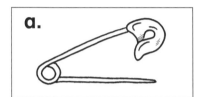   b.    c.

4. _____   a.    b.    c.

5. _____   a.    b.    c.

6. _____   a.    b.    c.

7. _____   a. 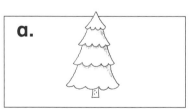   b. 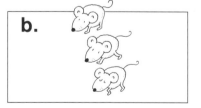   c.

8. _____   a.    b. 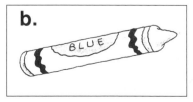   c.

Unit 1

Fill in the blanks.

1. _____girls' room_____

2. _____

3. _____

4. _____

5. _____

6. _____

7. _____

8. _____

8

Fill in the blanks.

| your | across | I'm | Come | name's | Excuse | lunchroom |

1. ___Excuse___ me. Where's the _____ ?

    It's _____ from the gym.

2. _____ with me.

    OK.

3. My _____ Amy. What's _____ name?

    _____ David.

Look at page 8, read, and write.

1. Where's the girls' room? (across from)
It's across from the music room._____

2. Where's the office? (next to)

_____

3. Where's the library? (next to)

_____

4. Where's the classroom? (across from)

_____

Look and match.

1. 100	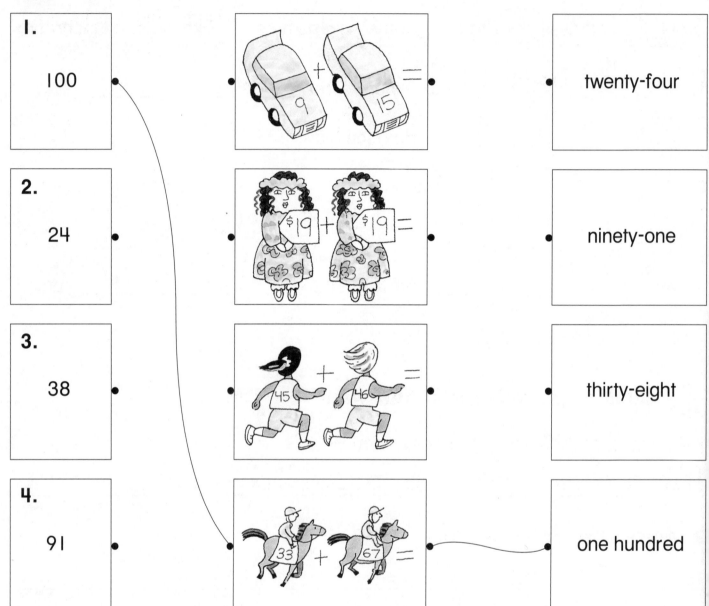	twenty-four
2. 24		ninety-one
3. 38		thirty-eight
4. 91		one hundred

 Look and write.

1. 20   40   **60**   80   _____sixty_____

2. _____   30   40   50   _____

3. 55   60   65   _____   _____

10

Look and write.

1.
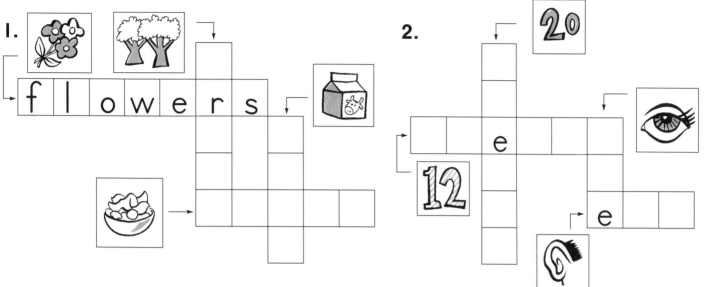

f l o w e r s

2.

B **Choose and write.**

___b___ 1. I have a _____key_____ in my bag.

   a. stove   **b.** key   **c.** bicycle

_____ 2. There is _____ near the lamp.

   a. trees   **b.** an ear   **c.** a telephone

_____ 3. She is my _____.

   a. police officer **b.** nurse   **c.** mother

_____ 4. I'm thirsty. I want _____.

   a. a hamburger **b.** milk   **c.** a robot

11

Read and write.

1.

This is Amy's house. It has a kitchen, a living room, a bathroom, a dining room, and three bedrooms.

How many rooms are there?

There are seven rooms.

2.

7	17	27	37
47	57	★	67
70	71	72	73
74	76	77	78

Look at these numbers. Count the sevens.

How many sevens are there?

_____

3.

These are flowers. They are red, yellow, and purple.

How many flowers are there?

_____

4.

These are Wendy's friends. They are Ben, Amy, and David.

How many friends does Wendy have?

_____

Listen and write a ✓ or an ✗. 🔲

1.

2.

3.

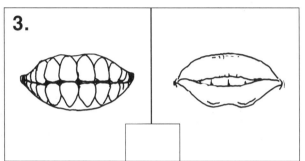

4.

 Listen and write. 🔲

1.

t h r e e

2.

__ o ___ er

3.

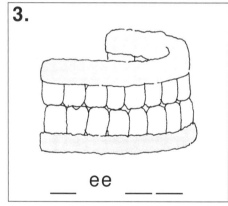

__ ee ____

4.

__ a ___ er

5.

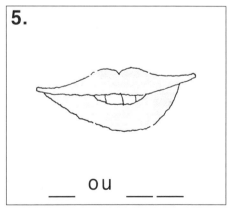

__ ou ____

6.

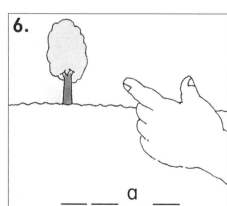

____ a ___

Match and write.

1. __Who's__ in the lunchroom? (Who's, Where's)

Roy's in the lunchroom.

2. _____ Kim? (Who's, Where's)

_____

3. _____ in the boys' room? (Who's, Where's)

_____

4. _____ Amy? (Who's, Where's)

_____

14

Listen and write a ✓. 🔲

1.

2.

3.

4.

 Listen, write, and circle.

1. __70__	seven	seventeen	(seventy)
2. _____	four	fourteen	forty
3. _____	six	sixteen	sixty
4. _____	five	fifteen	fifty
5. _____	nine	nineteen	ninety

15

Unit 2

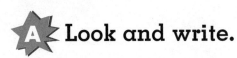 **Look and write.**

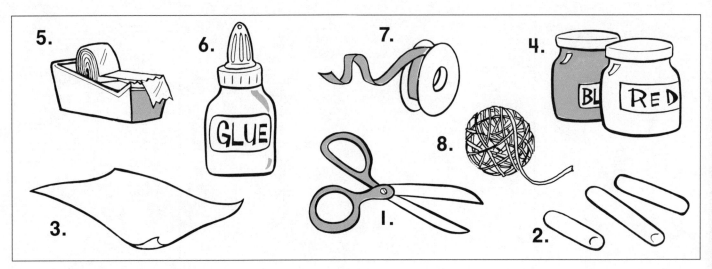

1. ___scissors___

2. _____

3. _____

4. _____

5. _____

6. _____

7. _____

8. _____

B **Read and choose.**

__b__ 1. Do you have any green paper?

   a. No, thanks.

   b. No, I don't. Sorry.

_____ 2. Here you are.

   a. Thank you.

   b. Yes, please.

_____ 3. Do you want some?

   a. Yes, please.

   b. No, I don't. Sorry.

Look and write.

1.		What do you have? I have some paper.
2.		What do you have? _____
3.		What do you have? _____

 Read, choose, and write.

1. Do you have any (tape) / paint ?

No, ____I____ ___don't___ .

2. Do you have any paper / glue ?

Yes, _____ _____ .

3. Do you have any chalk / string ?

No, _____ _____ .

4. Do you have any tape / ribbon ?

Yes, _____ _____ .

Look and write.

 They have some paint, but they don't have any paper.

_____

_____

_____

_____

_____

_____

B **Unscramble the sentences.**

1. doesn't / She / any / glue / have / .

She doesn't have any glue.

2. some / have / paper / They / .

_____

3. string / any / don't / I / have / .

_____

Look, read, and write.

1. __What does she have_____?

She has some chalk.

2. __Do they_____?

Yes, they do. They have some tape.

3. _____?

No, he doesn't. He doesn't have any string.

4. _____?

They have some scissors.

5. _____?

Yes, she does. She has some paint.

6. _____?

He has some ribbon.

A **Read and draw.**

1. a square	**2.** a circle
3. a triangle	**4.** a rectangle

 B **Read and write.**

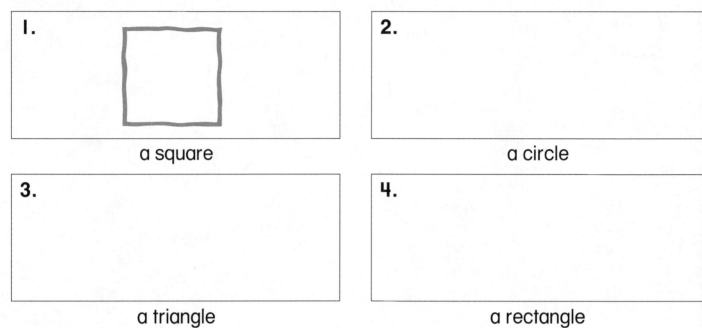

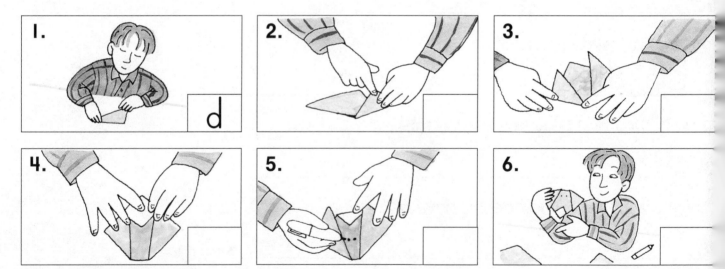

a. Fold this corner and make a triangle. This is a nose.

b. What is it? It's a dog.

c. Fold this corner and make a triangle. This is an ear.

d. Fold the paper and make a triangle.

e. Draw two circles. These are eyes.

f. Fold this corner and make a triangle. This is an ear, too.

Listen and circle.

1.

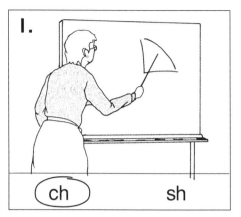

(ch)   sh

2.

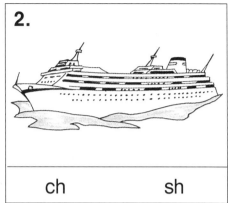

ch   sh

3.

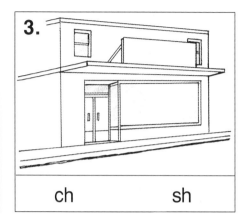

ch   sh

4.

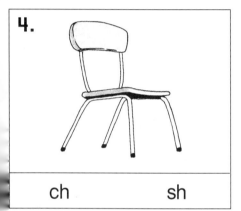

ch   sh

5.

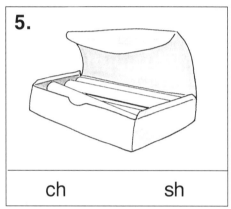

ch   sh

6.

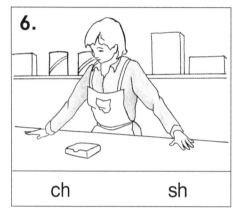

ch   sh

 Listen and circle.

1.

<u>sh</u>ip

a.   b.   c.   d.   e.

2.

<u>ch</u>air

a.   b.   c.   d.   e.

21

Unscramble the sentences.

1. any / Sue / have / glue / doesn't / .

Sue doesn't have any glue.

2. bird / has / Sue / a / .

_____

3. isn't / But / happy / Sue / .

_____

4. string / some / has / Sue / .

_____

B **Look and write.**

1. Does Sue have any glue?

No, she doesn't.

2. What does she have?

_____

3. Is she happy?

_____

Listen and write a ✓. 🔲

		GLUE	✂	▱	PAINT	🧶
I.						✔
2.						
3.						
4.						
5.						

 Listen and circle. 🔲

1.
a. Does she have any paint? (circled)
b. Does she have any markers?

2.
a. Do they have any ribbon?
b. Do they have any chalk?

3.
a. Does he have any scissors?
b. Does he have any string?

Review Unit

 A **Read and choose.**

_c_ 1. <u>Excuse me.</u> Where's the gym?

   a. Please.   **b.** Thank you.   **c.** Excuse me.

_____ 2. _____. OK.

   a. What's your name? **b.** Come with me.   **c.** This is David.

_____ 3. Do you want some? _____.

   a. Yes, please.   **b.** Sorry.   **c.** Here you are.

_____ 4. Do you have _____ green paper?

   a. some   **b.** any   **c.** want

 B **Read, circle, and write.**

1.

Do you have any glue / (tape) ?

Yes, <u>I do.</u> .

2.

Do you have any chalk / paper ?

No, _____.

3.

Do you have any string / ribbon ?

No, _____.

4.

Do you have any markers / paint ?

Yes, _____.

Listen and match. 🔲

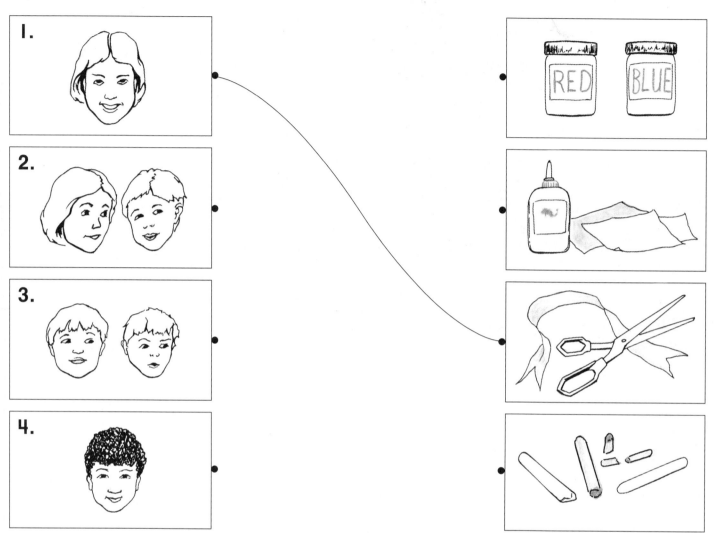

1.

2.

3.

4.

 Listen, read, and match. 🔲

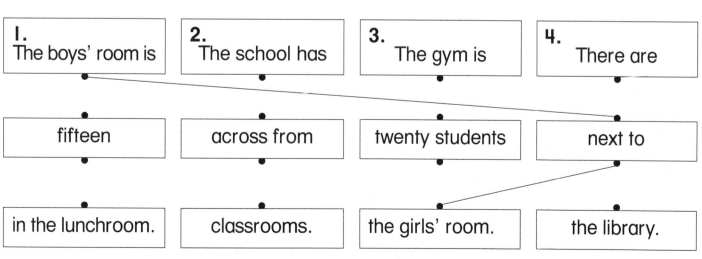

1. The boys' room is	2. The school has	3. The gym is	4. There are
fifteen	across from	twenty students	next to
in the lunchroom.	classrooms.	the girls' room.	the library.

25

Unit 3

 Read and arrange.

1. __f__	**a.** Sunday's OK. I'm free.
2. _____	**b.** What do you do?
3. _____	**c.** Oh. What about Sunday? Are you busy?
4. _____	**d.** Sorry. I can't. I'm busy every Saturday.
5. _____	**e.** Great! See you on Sunday!
6. _____	**f.** Can you play with us tomorrow?
7. _____	**g.** I go to my grandmother's house.

B **Read and write.**

Tuesday	Saturday	Monday	Thursday	Sunday

Friday	Wednesday

1. Sunday

2. _____

3. _____

4. _____

5. _____

6. _____

7. _____

Look and write.

1. piano class

2. _____

3. _____

4. _____

5. _____

6. _____

B **Read and write.**

Sunday	My grandmother's house
Monday	Art class
Tuesday	Piano class
Wednesday	English class
Thursday	Math class
Friday	Computer class
Saturday	Swimming class

1. What do you do on Friday?

I go to computer class.

2. What do you do on Monday?

_____

3. What do you do on Saturday?

_____

4. What do you do on Wednesday?

_____

Read and match.

1. play	2. practice	3. take	4. watch	5. go

TV	a nap	video games	to the bookstore	the piano

 Rewrite the sentences.

1. <u>David studies</u> English after school. (I)

   <u>I study English after school.</u>

2. Every day <u>she sings</u> at school. (we)

   _____

3. <u>Ben and Wendy like</u> sports. (Wendy)

   _____

4. What <u>does he do</u> after school? (you)

   _____

Read and write.

What does he do after school?

He watches TV.

What do they do after school?

_____

What does she do after school?

_____

 Make questions.

1. Does he practice the piano after school?

No, he doesn't. He doesn't practice the piano.

2. _____

Yes, I do. I go to the bookstore.

3. _____

No, they don't. They don't play soccer.

4. _____

Yes, she does. She does her homework.

Read and write.

1.  This is Meg. Her favorite day is Wednesday. She goes to karate class with her brother.

What is Meg's favorite day?

Her favorite day is Wednesday.

Where does she go on Wednesday?

_____

Does she go with her father?

_____

2.  This is Sam. His favorite day is Saturday. He plays basketball with his friends.

What is Sam's favorite day?

_____

Does he stay at home on Saturday?

_____

What does he do?

_____

30

Listen and write *pl* or *bl*.

1.  `bl`	**2.** 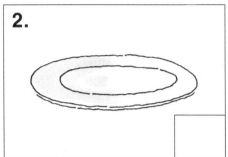	**3.** 
4. 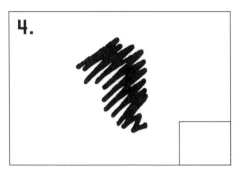	**5.** 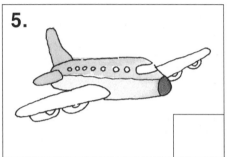	**6.** 

 Listen and choose the word with the different sound.

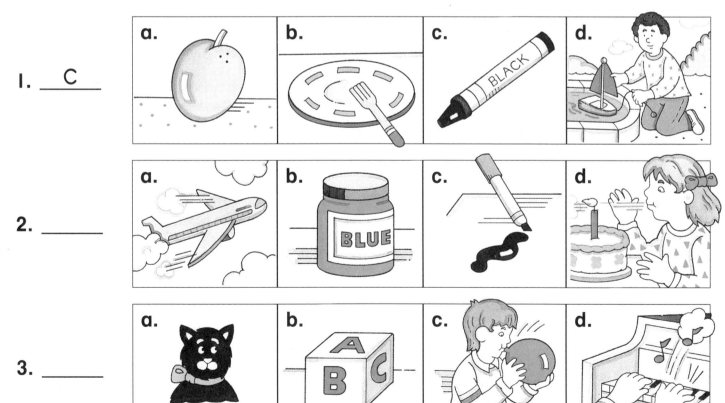

1. ___C___

2. _____

3. _____

Look, read, and write.

	Sunday	Monday	Tuesday	Wednesday	Thursday	Friday	Saturday
David	free		free		math class		swimming class
Jenny		karate class		free	computer class	free	
Wendy	piano class	free		dance class			free
John		free	English class		free	art class	
you							

1. Is Jenny free on Monday?

No, she isn't.

2. What does Wendy do on Sunday?

_____

3. Is John busy on Tuesday?

_____

4. Where does David go on Thursday?

_____

5. What day is your free day?

_____

6. What do you do on Wednesday?

_____

Listen and circle.

1. Saturday

(Yes, he does.)

No, he doesn't.

2. Tuesday

Yes, she is.

No, she isn't.

3. Thursday

Yes, he does.

No, he doesn't.

4. Sunday

Yes, she is.

No, she isn't.

Listen and match.

1.	2.	3.	4.	5.
	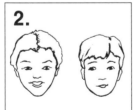	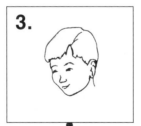		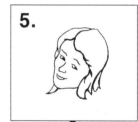
	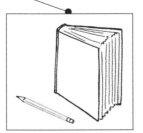		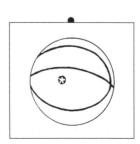	

Unit 4

 Fill in the blanks.

tomorrow	time	OK	too	late

sorry	At	hungry	dinner	eat

I'm ___hungry___ .
1.

Me, _____ . When do you _____ dinner?
2.   3.

_____ 5:30. What _____ is it now?
4.   5.

It's 5:45.

Oh, no! I'm _____ . Bye!
6.

See you _____ !
7.

I'm _____ I'm late.
8.

That's _____ . Here's your _____ .
9.   10.

 Read and draw.

I. It's five thirty. It's half past five. 	**2.** It's five forty-five. It's a quarter to six. 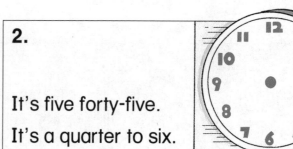

A **Look and write.**

1. It's two fifteen.
It's a quarter after two.

2. _____

3. _____

4. _____

 B **Look, read, and write.**

1.
9:45

When does he go to bed?
He goes to bed at 9:45.

2.
6:30

When do they eat dinner?
_____

3.
7:00

When does she get up?
_____

Look, read, and write.

	always	usually	sometimes	never
	Ben	Wendy	Amy	David

1. Ben always rides his bicycle to school.

2. _____

3. _____

4. _____

B Look, read, and match.

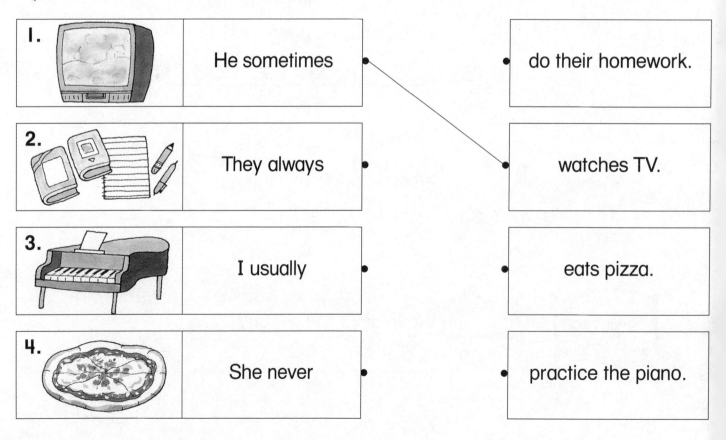

1.	He sometimes	•	•	do their homework.
2.	They always	•	•	watches TV.
3.	I usually	•	•	eats pizza.
4.	She never	•	•	practice the piano.

Read and write.

	(video games)	(soccer)	(nap)	(pizza)
1.				sometimes
2.			usually	
3.		always		
4.	never			

1. Do they ever eat pizza?

Yes, they sometimes eat pizza.

2. Does he ever take a nap?

_____

3. Do they ever play soccer?

_____

4. Does she ever play video games?

_____

5. Do you ever play soccer?

_____

6. Do you ever take a nap?

_____

A Read and write.

| every | morning | After | Sometimes | very | always |

1. Jeff is <u>v e r y</u> busy every day.

2. He goes to school early in the ___ ___ ___ ___ ___ ___ ___ .

3. ___ ___ ___ ___ ___ school he rides his bicycle.

4. ___ ___ ___ ___ ___ ___ ___ ___ ___ he plays soccer with his friends.

5. He ___ ___ ___ ___ ___ ___ does his homework in the evening.

6. He goes to sleep at 10:00 ___ ___ ___ ___ ___ night.

B Now answer these questions.

1. When does Jeff go to school?

   <u>He goes to school early in the morning.</u>

2. Does he ever play soccer after school?

   _____

3. What does he do in the evening?

   _____

4. What time does he go to sleep?

   _____

Listen and match.

1.

2.

3.

cl   gl

4.

5.
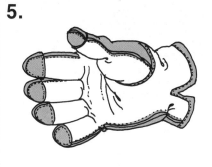

6.
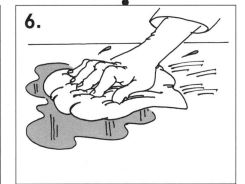

 Listen and write *cl* **or** *gl*.

1.

Please __c__ __l__ ean the ___ ___ ock

in the ___ ___ assroom.

2.

There is ___ ___ ue on this ___ ___ ass

and this ___ ___ ove.

39

Read and match.

1. It's four o'clock.	It's 4:15.
2. It's a quarter to four.	It's 4:30.
3. It's half past four.	It's 3:45.
4. It's a quarter after four.	It's 4:00.

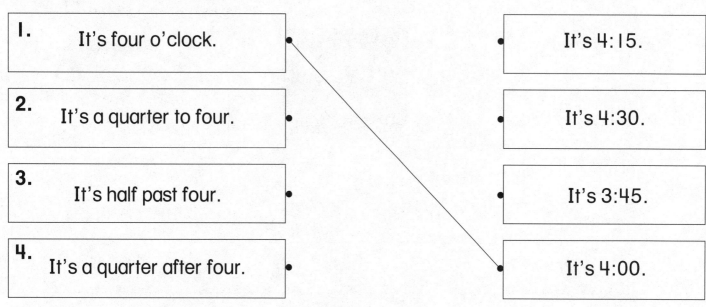

 Look, read, and write.

He usually goes to school at 8:30.

Is he late?

Yes, he is.

She usually goes to English class at 4:00.

Is she late?

_____

They usually go to karate class at 7:15.

Are they late?

_____

Listen and draw.

1.

2.
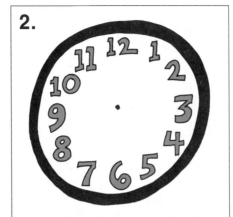

3.

4.

5.
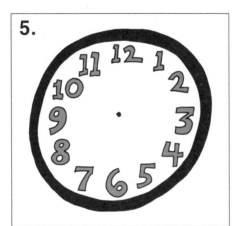

6.
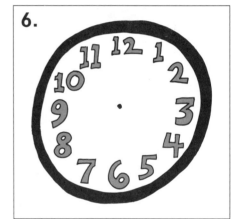

B Listen and match.

1. David	always	eats dinner at 6:15.
2. Wendy	usually	eats breakfast at 7:30.
3. Ben	sometimes	eats lunch at 2:00.
4. Amy	never	eats pizza for lunch.

41

Review Unit

 A **Read and match.**

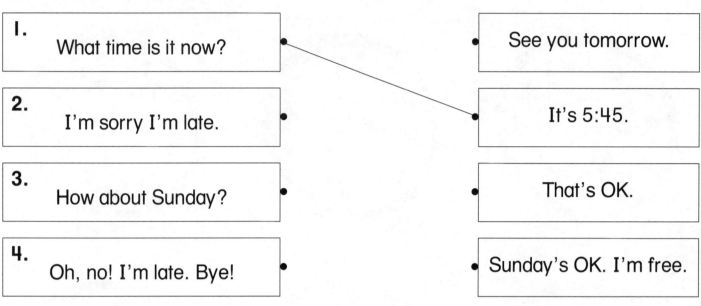

1. What time is it now?	See you tomorrow.
2. I'm sorry I'm late.	It's 5:45.
3. How about Sunday?	That's OK.
4. Oh, no! I'm late. Bye!	Sunday's OK. I'm free.

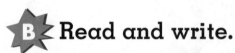 **B** **Read and write.**

1. Do you ever do homework in the evening?

Yes, I usually do homework in the evening.

2. What time do you get up?

_____

3. When do you go to English class?

_____

4. Are you free on Saturday?

_____

5. What's your favorite day?

_____

42

Listen and circle.

1. **a.** No, he doesn't.
   b. No, he isn't.

2. **a.** She gets up early.
   b. She gets up at 6:30.

3. **a.** They play soccer.
   b. They eat breakfast.

4. **a.** I go to school.
   b. I watch TV.

 Listen and choose.

___a___ 1. Wendy goes to computer class on _____Monday_____.

   a. Monday   **b.** Tuesday   **c.** Thursday

_____ 2. She always goes at _____.

   a. 5:15   **b.** 5:30   **c.** 5:45

_____ 3. _____ she plays basketball with her friends.

   a. Always   **b.** Usually   **c.** Sometimes

_____ 4. Her favorite day is _____.

   a. Monday   **b.** Thursday   **c.** Sunday

Unit 5

 Unscramble the sentences.

1. one / the / like / green / I / .

   <u>I like the green one.</u>

2. this / mean / Do / one / you / ?

   _____

3. look / You / great / !

   _____

4. do / like / Which / you / one/ ?

   _____

 Read and write.

1. I like the green dress. ⟶ <u>I like the green one.</u>

2. He likes the big dog. ⟶ _____

3. They like the round kite. ⟶ _____

4. She likes the small eraser. ⟶ _____

5. You like the white hat. ⟶ _____

44

Look and write.

1.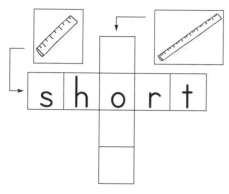

s h o r t

2.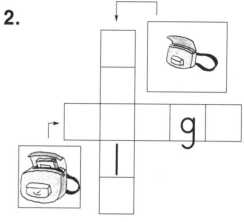

g

3.

r

k o

d

4.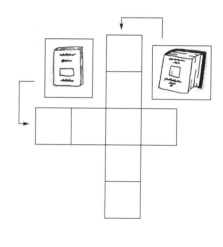

 Look, read, and write.

1.

Which bag do you like?

I like the large one.

2.

Which car do you like?

45

Look, write, and circle.

1.
c <u>o</u> <u>a</u> t

2.
b _ _ _ _ e

3.
s _ _ _ t

4.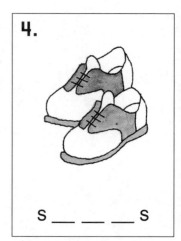
s _ _ _ s

5.
j _ _ _ s

6.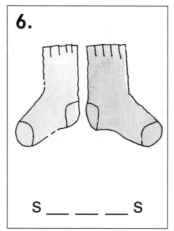
s _ _ _ s

7.
b _ _ _ s

8.
s _ _ _ _ r

b	o	o	t	s	z	i	f	p	e	o	s
l	p	z	h	w	p	a	j	a	w	z	s
o	r	b	j	e	l	x	e	w	d	b	h
u	t	c	o	a	t	h	a	b	z	w	o
s	k	i	r	t	q	n	n	z	y	r	e
e	v	f	k	e	r	v	s	o	c	k	s
w	x	g	m	r	x	c	s	h	i	m	t

Look, match, and write.

1.	2.	3.
striped sweaters jeans	black skirt boots	white T-shirt polka dot shorts

1. What's she wearing?

<u>She's wearing a black skirt and boots.</u>

Is she wearing a coat?

_____

2. What's he wearing?

_____

Is he wearing socks?

_____

3. What are they wearing?

_____

Are they wearing shoes?

_____

Fill in the blanks.

1. It's r <u>a i n i n g</u>. Ann has
an u __ __ __ __ __ __ a. She's wearing
yellow b __ __ __ s. She is
j __ __ __ __ __ g in a puddle.

2. The sun is s __ __ __ __ __ g. It's a
h __ t day. Tim is w __ __ __ __ __ g
shorts and a T-shirt. He is
c __ __ __ __ __ __ g a tree.

3. It's s __ __ __ __ __ g. It's a very
c __ __ d day. Sue and Jim are wearing
c __ __ __ s and mittens. They are
t __ __ __ __ __ __ g snowballs.

4. The wind is b __ __ __ __ __ g. It's
a w __ __ __ y day. Dan and Kim are
wearing j __ __ __ __ __ s. They
are f __ __ __ __ g kites.

Listen and write. 📼

1.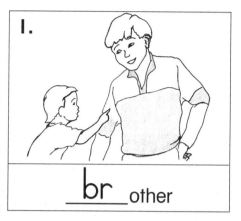

_br_other

2.

_____incess

3.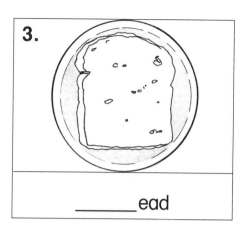

_____ead

4.

_____esent

5.

_____eakfast

6.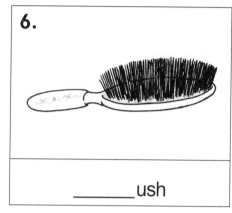

_____ush

 Listen and write. 📼

1.

The __pr__ince is _____ushing

the _____own dog.

2.

My _____other is giving

the _____incess a _____esent.

49

Read, match, and color.

1.

The kids are wearing black shorts, yellow T-shirts, and orange socks.

2.

The girls are wearing red T-shirts, purple skirts, and yellow socks.

3.

The boys are wearing blue jeans, green sweaters, and black sneakers.

Listen and write. 📼

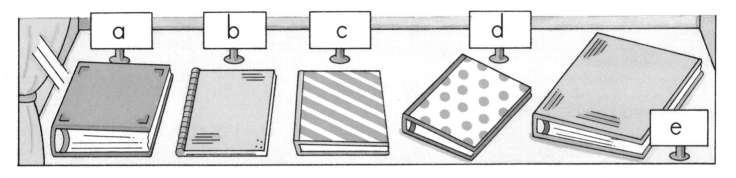

1. __C__   2. _____   3. _____   4. _____   5. _____

 Listen and match. 📼

1.	2.	3.	4.
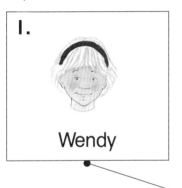 Wendy	 David	 Amy	 Ben

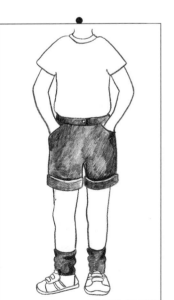   

Unit 6

A Read and match.

1. Oh, Wendy! Let me help you.

2. Are you going to the post office?

3. Where are you going?

4. See you later, Amy. Thanks for helping me.

No, I'm not.

I'm going to the library.

You're welcome. Bye!

Thanks, Amy.

B Unscramble the sentences.

1. going / you / the / Are / post / to / office / ?

Are you going to the post office?

2. me / Thanks / helping / for / .

_____

3. to / going / the / I'm / library / .

_____

Look and write.

  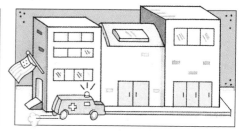

1. <u>supermarket</u>   2. _____   3. _____

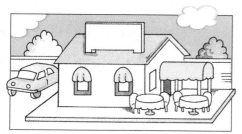 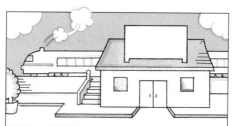 

4. _____   5. _____   6. _____

 Look, read, and write.

Where are you going?

1. <u>We're going to school.</u>

2. _____

3. _____

Look, read, and write.

1. Where is Ben's mother going?

She's going to the supermarket.

2. How is she going there?

_____

3. Where are Ben and Amy going?

_____

4. Is Wendy going to the library?

_____

5. How is she going there?

_____

54

Read and choose.

___C___ **1.** They're _____taking_____ a bus.

      a. driving   **b.** walking   **c.** taking

_____ **2.** He's going to the _____.

      a. home   **b.** hospital   **c.** school

_____ **3.** She's _____ a car.

      a. driving   **b.** riding   **c.** taking

_____ **4.** They're riding _____.

      a. cars   **b.** taxis   **c.** bicycles

_____ **5.** She's going _____.

      a. library   **b.** home   **c.** school

B **Read and write.**

1. Where are they going? _____

They're going to the department store.

2. _____

She's walking.

3. _____

No, he isn't. He's going to the restaurant.

4. _____

I'm going to the supermarket.

Look, read, and write.

Brazil

France

Canada

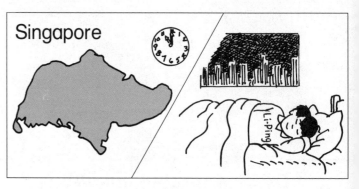
Singapore

1. What time is it in France?

_____

2. Does Marta live in Canada?

_____

3. What is Li-Ping doing?

_____

4. Where does Sally live?

_____

5. Do Pierre and Marie live in France?

_____

6. What time is it in Singapore?

_____

56

Listen and write a ✓ or an X.

1.

✓

2.

3.

4.

 Listen and choose the word with the different sound.

1.   __C__

   a.  **b.** **c.**

2.   _____

   a.  **b.** **c.**

3.   _____

   a.  **b.** **c.**

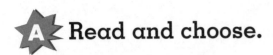 **Read and choose.**

| a. I speak English. | b. I eat dinner. |
| c. I play baseball. | d. I look at the books. |

__d__ 1. What do you do in the bookstore?

_____ 2. What do you do in English class?

_____ 3. What do you do at the park?

_____ 4. What do you do at the restaurant?

B Read and write.

1. Where are you going? (park)

   To the park.

   What do you do there? (ride my bicycle)

   I ride my bicycle.

2. Where are you going? (department store)

   _____

   What do you do there? (look at the dresses)

   _____

3. Where are you going? (school)

   _____

   What do you do there? (listen to my teacher)

   _____

Listen and match.

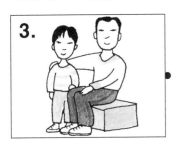

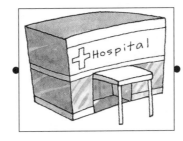

 Listen and choose.

___b___ **1.** **a.** Yes, they do.

b. Yes, they are.

c. Yes, they can.

_____ **2.** **a.** To the park.

b. Yes, she does.

c. In Canada.

_____ **3.** **a.** Yes, it is.

b. No, it doesn't.

c. It's 3:00.

_____ **4.** **a.** He lives in Singapore.

b. He studies English.

c. He is sleeping.

59

Review Unit

 A Read and write.

| mean | one | Let | helping | Which |

1. Thank you for _____ **helping** _____ me.

2. _____ hat do you like?

3. Do you _____ this one?

4. _____ me help you.

5. No, the big _____ .

B Look and write.

| 1. | 2. | 3. | 4. |

Which one do you like?

1. I like the long one. _____

2. _____

3. _____

4. _____

Listen and write.

1. e	2.	3.	4.	5.

a. They're wearing sweaters and jeans.

b. No, I'm walking.

c. I'm riding my bicycle.

d. I'm wearing shorts and a T-shirt.

e. He's going to school.

 Listen and write a ✓ or an ✗.

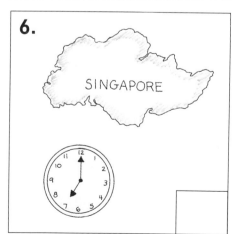

Unit 7

 Read and write.

1. e	2.	3.	4.	5.	6.

a. It was great.

b. Wow! They're big!

c. I was at the museum.

d. There were some big dinosaurs. Look at these pictures.

e. Hi, Ben. Where were you yesterday?

f. How was it?

 Unscramble the sentences.

1. it / How / was / ?

How was it?

2. the / I / at / museum / was / .

_____

3. you / yesterday / were / Where / ?

_____

4. We / beach / were / the / at / .

_____

Read and write.

1. I am at the beach. ⟶ <u>I was at the beach.</u>

2. How is it? ⟶ _____

3. Where are you? ⟶ _____

4. It is fun. ⟶ _____

5. We are at the museum. ⟶ _____

 Look and write.

amusement park
HOUSE OF MIRR
fun

Where were you yesterday?
<u>I was at the amusement park.</u>
How was it?
<u>It was fun.</u>

zoo
great

Where were you yesterday?
_____
How was it?
_____

swimming pool
fun

Where were you yesterday?
_____
How was it?
_____

Read and circle.

1. I (was) on the slide.
   were

2. You was at the playground.
        were

3. Amy and Ben was at the zoo.
                were

4. Wendy was on the jungle gym.
          were

5. He was at the beach.
       were

 Read and choose.

__c__ 1. David _____was_____ on the slide.

        a. are   **b.** were   **c.** was

_____ 2. Now he _____ on the seesaw.

        a. was   **b.** is   **c.** were

_____ 3. They _____ at the museum yesterday.

        a. were   **b.** are   **c.** was

_____ 4. Now they _____ at the swimming pool.

        a. were   **b.** are   **c.** was

Look, read, and write.

1.

Where's he now?

He's on the swing.

Where was he?

_____

Was he on the slide?

_____

2.

Where are they now?

_____

Where were they?

_____

Were they on the swings?

_____

3.

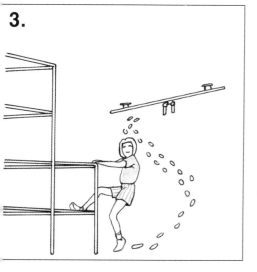

Where's she now?

_____

Where was she?

_____

Was she on the slide?

_____

A ★ Look and write.

| c | a | t | e | r | p | i | l | l | a | r |

| | | |
| | d | |

| | |
| | e |

p

B ★ Look, read, and write.

1.

What was it before?

<u>It was a tadpole.</u>

2.

What were they before?

_____

3.

What was it before?

_____

Listen and circle.

1. 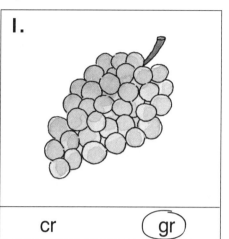	2. 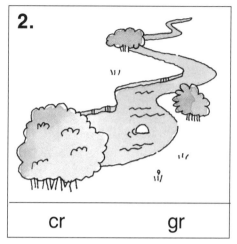	3. 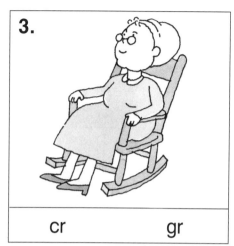
cr (gr)	cr gr	cr gr

4. 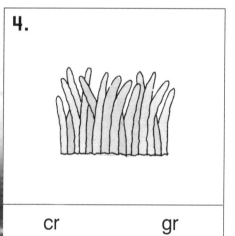	5. 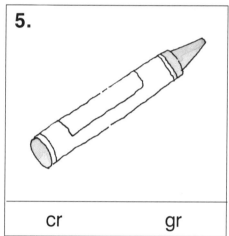	6. 
cr gr	cr gr	cr gr

 Listen and write cr or gr.

1.

The __c__ __r__ ocodile is eating ___ ___ een ___ ___ apes.

2.

A ___ ___ ane is in the ___ ___ ass near a ___ ___ eek.

67

Read and match.

1. Where were you at two?

They were here all day.

2. Where was she at three?

I was at the zoo.

3. Where were they at four?

I was on a great big rock.

4. Where were you at five o'clock?

They were at the store.

5. Where were Jack and Ray?

She was in a tree.

Listen and write a ✓ or an ✗.

 Listen and write.

I. d	2.	3.	4.

a. She was at the swimming pool.

b. I was at the museum.

c. They were at the zoo.

d. He was at the amusement park.

Unit 8

 Read and choose.

__b__ **1.** Let's ___give___ it to the teacher.

    a. find   **b.** give   **c.** was

_____ **2.** I _____ a wallet!

    a. found   **b.** can't   **c.** give

_____ **3.** Really? Where _____ it?

    a. find   **b.** was   **c.** found

_____ **4.** I can't _____ my wallet.

    a. look   **b.** give   **c.** find

B **Read and match.**

1. Let's give it to the teacher.

2. I can't find my wallet.

3. Really? Where was it?

4. Where is it now?

Hey, I found a wallet.

We gave it to the teacher.

Good idea.

It was under the slide.

Look, read, and write.

1. What did she find?

She found a coin.

Where was it?

_____

2. Did they find a ball?

_____

Was it in a puddle?

_____

3. Did he find a wallet?

_____

What did he find?

_____

4. Was it in the tree?

_____

Where was it?

_____

Look, read, and write.

1.

Wendy went to the c i r c u s

yesterday. She saw t ___ ___ ___ ___ s and

b ___ ___ ___ s. She ate p ___ ___ ___ ___ ___ n.

She drank s ___ ___ a p ___ p.

It was fun.

2.

Ben and Amy w ___ ___ t to the circus, too.

They saw m ___ ___ ___ ___ ___ s and

e ___ ___ ___ ___ ___ ___ ___ s. They ate

f ___ ___ ___ ___ h f ___ ___ ___ s and i ___ e

c ___ ___ ___ m. They drank w ___ ___ ___ r.

It was fun.

3.

David went to the c ___ ___ ___ ___ s, too. He

s ___ w tigers and monkeys. He a ___ e cotton

candy. He d ___ ___ ___ k lemonade. It was fun.

Write.

1. go → <u>going</u> → <u>went</u>

2. see → _____ → _____

3. eat → _____ → _____

4. drink → _____ → _____

 Look, read, and write.

1.

What did she drink?

<u>She drank soda pop.</u>

2.

What did you see?

_____

3.

What did he eat?

_____

4.

What did they drink?

_____

73

Unscramble the sentences.

1. Saturday / museum / went / a / Alan / Last / to / .

<u>Last Saturday Alan went to a museum.</u>

2. some / She / a / french fries / ate / hot dog / and / .

_____

3. pictures / these / took / They / .

_____

4. went / had / swimming / and / picnic / a / They / .

_____

 Read and write.

What did he see?

He saw rockets and airplanes.

_____

She ate french fries and ice cream.

_____

They went to an amusement park.

Listen and match.

1.

2.

3.

fr	fl

4.

5.

6.

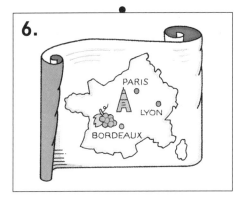

 Listen and write a ✓ or an ✗.

1.

fr

a. ✔   b. _____   c. _____

2.

fl

a. _____   b. _____   c. _____

75

A **Read and write.**

What	Where	Who

1. ____What____ did you find? A flea.

2. _____ did they go? To L.A.

3. _____ did he see? His Aunt Marie.

4. _____ did she drink? A cup of tea.

B **Read and match.**

1. What did you eat?		I went at three.
2. How was the fish?		She said, "Hi."
3. When did you go?		It was delicious.
4. What did she say?		I ate some fish.

Listen and draw.

1. 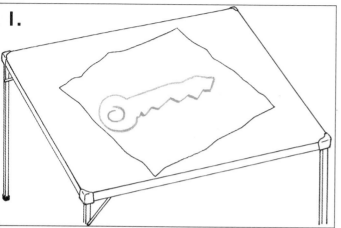	**2.** 
3. 	**4.** 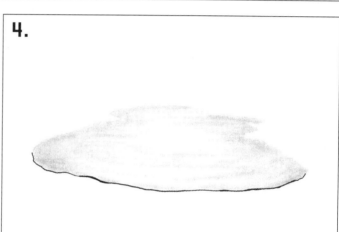

B **Listen and write a ✓ or an ✗.**

✗   **1.** Amy and Ben went to the zoo.

_____ **2.** They saw tigers and bears.

_____ **3.** They ate french fries and ice cream.

_____ **4.** They drank some soda pop.

_____ **5.** It was fun!

Review Unit

 A Read, choose, and write.

> **a.** We gave it to the teacher.   **b.** I was at the museum.
>
> **c.** It was great.   **d.** Hey, I found a wallet!

_c_ **1.** How was it? _It was great._

____ **2.** I can't find my wallet. _____

____ **3.** Where were you yesterday? _____

____ **4.** Where is it now? _____

 B Look, read, and write.

Where was she?

She was on the jungle gym.

_____

No, he wasn't. He was not at the beach.

_____

They were on the seesaw.

_____

Yes, I was. I was at the zoo.

Listen and match.

1.

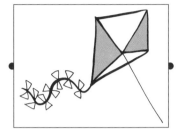

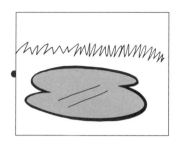

2.

3.

4.

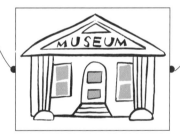

5.

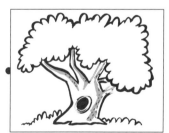

6.